Lifecharge
Organizational PowerPAC

Principles, Applications and Charts

By

Scott L. Newberger MBA, MA, CMC

Where there is no vision, the people perish
- Proverbs 29:18

Table of Contents

How to use this book

In today's fast paced world, where change happens quickly and frequently, time is at a premium. Yet, organizations must remain diligent in being innovative to keep up with the increasing pace of technology while staying dedicated to vision and mission. For an organization to survive and thrive in such an environment, continual analysis and progress towards relevant goals is essential. This book may be considered a guide or handbook to provide direction and practical applications for organizations to develop and focus on their core purpose while remaining flexible with changing conditions.

The book is arranged in bullet format with applications for each concept, as well as charts and worksheets to facilitate rapid comprehension of principles. It can be read from front to back, immediately or over time, while completing related activities along the way. This may be the most effective way for members to complete a comprehensive analysis of their organization and then set and achieve goals that are important. However, it can also be used as a reference book to learn about certain principles when desired and to complete activities that can help one grasp individual concepts and cultivate new skills.

Worksheets are designed to facilitate learning by applying principles directly to one's own circumstances. When completing worksheets, ample space is provided to fill in each field completely. However, filling in each field is not necessary to benefit from using the worksheet. Individuals can fill in some of the fields or use the worksheets as desired to learn and apply principles as each situation demands. The worksheets can be revisited later for further completion or new worksheets may be started based on new information.

This book was created to provide a quick and comprehensive way for organizations to learn to examine their structure, define a mission and vision, as well as formulate and achieve meaningful goals. It is hoped that all who learn from it may grow and help their organization reach a self defined high level of achievement.

POWER PRINCIPLES

POWER PRINCIPLE 1:

Each organization has inherent worth and possesses potential.

- Absolute essential initial principle to which members of an organization must gain a conviction as it will be the foundation for the integration and development of all other principles.

- A realization of inherent characteristic strengths, resources and opportunities is an important element of this principle.

- Some organizations are restricted by incorrect assumptions of the vision and mission of the organization.

- An appreciation of the positive aspects of an organization assists its management in discovering and creating strengths that will help the organization succeed.

Application:

Create list of positive qualities your organization. Refrain from including negative aspects at this time. There will be an opportunity to consider those during analysis.

Powerful Positives

Create a list of your organizations positive qualities and attributes.

_____
_____
_____
_____
_____
_____
_____
_____
_____
_____
_____
_____
_____
_____
_____
_____
_____
_____
_____
_____
_____
_____
_____
_____
_____

POWER PRINCIPLE 2:

Organizations have the power to change, progress and use their resources to create the future they desire.

- There are opportunities *now* that can affect the future.

- Each organization has the characteristics and resources to meet with opportunities to achieve some level of success.

- Despite past performance or accomplishments, an organization has the power to accomplish and become what once may have been considered impossible.

- **Now** is the time to begin. Organizations need to embrace positive change now!

Application:

Identify traditionally held beliefs, patterns of behavior, practices and policies that inhibit new growth or change within your organization. Consider if such may be modified or deleted to encourage progress and positive change.

Challenge for Change

Make a list of traditionally held beliefs, patterns of thought, assumptions and behaviors that inhibit new growth or change. Check each box when the perspective has changed or the item has been challenged.

☐ _____

_____

☐ _____

_____

☐ _____

_____

☐ _____

_____

☐ _____

_____

☐ _____

_____

☐ _____

_____

☐ _____

_____

☐ _____

_____

☐ _____

_____

POWER PRINCIPLE 3:

The Whole Organization Theory

- Each organization is a complex entity, made up of intellectual/research and developmental, cultural, physical and ethical characteristics

    1. **Intellectual/research and developmental**- This characteristic deals with the underlying intellectual principles of an organization that defines its operational functions and purpose. It incorporates the concept upon which the organization's products or services were created to meet a need of a group or individual. It also encapsulates new technology and innovation that enables further evolution of the organization and its products or services.

    2. **Cultural**- The culture of an organization refers to the shared attitudes, ideals, objectives, and behavior patterns that characterize that institution. The culture of the organization is manifest by its members through their interaction with others in and out of the organization, and through their dealings with their environment.

    3. **Physical**- Physical aspects of an organization in respects to The Whole Organizational Theory may encompass any of its resources including land, buildings, capital or financial resources and inventory.

    4. **Ethical**- The ethics of an organization refers to beliefs of what is right and wrong that governs the principles of conduct of the entity.

- Each complex organization interacts with other organizations, individuals and its environment. Within The Whole Organizational Theory, these exchanges are usually referred to as interactions and are described in the following way:

  1. **Interaction with others**- Each organization has dealings with other organizations and individuals. This may include exchanges both within and outside the entity. Such interactions influence and affect all that are involved.

  2. **Interaction with the environment**- All organizations have an impact on and are impacted by their environment. It is important to understand such interrelationships and learn how to most effectively manage them.

- To progress, each organization should analyze some or all of their characteristics and interactions and use them when given opportunities to reach their objectives.

- The Whole Organizational characteristics and interactions relate to and interact with one another. The proper balance of these characteristics and the management of interactions with others and the environment help an organization to be more fulfilled and productive.

Application:

Study and understand the characteristics and interactions of The Whole Organizational Theory. Consider how they apply to your organization.

POWER PRINCIPLE 3:
The Whole Organization

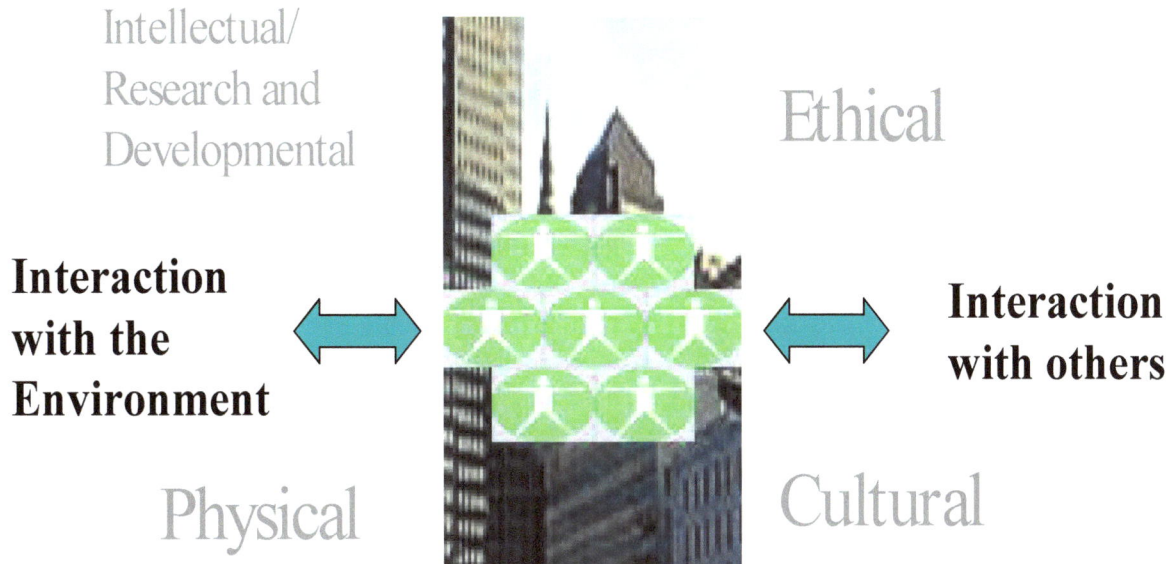

Intellectual/
Research and
Developmental

Ethical

**Interaction
with the
Environment**

**Interaction
with others**

Physical

Cultural

POWER PRINCIPLE 4:

Self Assessment through "SCODD Analysis"

- "SCODD Analysis"- Strengths, Challenges, Opportunities, Dangers and Desires

- Analysis of each characteristic and interaction of an organization should be based on the following:

- **Strengths**- Inherent or developed abilities of the organization that may be employed to reach the desire of the entity.

- **Challenges**- Inherent or developed shortcomings that could inhibit the achievement of the goals of the organization if not addressed, overcome or avoided.

  1. With diligence to improve, some challenges may be turned into strengths.

  2. Challenges should not be seen as things that would prohibit achieving or being what is desired. They should be viewed as obstacles to be overcome, improved upon or avoided.

  3. Each challenge should be analyzed to determine if it should be overcome and what it will take to do so, or if it should be avoided in order to accomplish the overall purpose.

- **Opportunities**- Occasions may arise, or be discovered in which strengths or desires may be maximized that will propel an organization towards achieving their overall purpose.

- **Dangers**- Risks or hazards that may inhibit the ability to use strengths to maximize opportunities. Such situations need to be identified and evaluated so appropriate action may be taken to minimize or eliminate the danger.

- **Desires**- It should be determined what's desired for the entity within each Whole Organizational characteristic and interaction.

    1. What is desired should be based on what is valued within each characteristic or interaction.

    2. Determining what's desired, based on what's valued, helps provide inherent motivation to achieve what is really important.

- A "SCODD Analysis" may be done for all or as many of the characteristics or interactions as desired to gain a good understanding of where an organization stands and what may need to be accomplished.

- "SCODD Analysis" may shed light on what is most important to an entity, and where it may be out of balance

Application:

Conduct a "SCODD Analysis" on any or all of the organizations characteristics and interactions.

"SCODD Analysis" Worksheet

INTELLECTUAL/RESEARCH AND DEVELOPMENTAL

Strengths: _____
_____
_____
_____

Challenges: _____
_____
_____
_____

Opportunities: _____
_____
_____
_____

Dangers: _____
_____
_____
_____

Desires: _____
_____
_____
_____

"SCODD Analysis" Worksheet

CULTURAL

Strengths: _____

_____

_____

_____

Challenges: _____

_____

_____

_____

Opportunities: _____

_____

_____

_____

Dangers: _____

_____

_____

_____

Desires: _____

_____

_____

_____

"SCODD Analysis" Worksheet
PHYSICAL

Strengths: _____

_____

_____

_____

Challenges: _____

_____

_____

_____

Opportunities: _____

_____

_____

_____

Dangers: _____

_____

_____

_____

Desires: _____

_____

_____

_____

"SCODD Analysis" Worksheet
ETHICAL

Strengths: _____
_____
_____
_____

Challenges: _____
_____
_____
_____

Opportunities: _____
_____
_____
_____

Dangers: _____
_____
_____
_____

Desires: _____
_____
_____
_____

"SCODD Analysis" Worksheet

INTERACTION WITH OTHERS

Strengths: _____

_____

_____

_____

Challenges: _____

_____

_____

_____

Opportunities: _____

_____

_____

_____

Dangers: _____

_____

_____

_____

Desires: _____

_____

_____

_____

"SCODD Analysis" Worksheet

INTERACTION WITH THE ENVIRONMENT

Strengths: _____

_____

_____

_____

Challenges: _____

_____

_____

_____

Opportunities: _____

_____

_____

_____

Dangers: _____

_____

_____

_____

Desires: _____

_____

_____

_____

POWER PRINCIPLE 5:

Based on the "SCODD Analysis," and organizational values, create a vision and mission statement. Then create and prioritize goals based on the vision and mission.

Vision Statement

- Defines what the organization is or will be.
- Short, succinct and easy to remember.
- Describes the organization in terms of strengths, opportunities and values.
- Should elicit a clear, graphic picture of the desired state of the organization.
- Helps to define the mission statement.
- Visions may change and adapt based on the time frame and current circumstances.

Mission Statement

- Clearly defines the organizations purpose.
- Explains how the entity will achieve its vision using strengths, opportunities and desire.
- Describes what will be employed to achieve the goal.

Application:

Create both a vision and mission statement for your organization.

Mission and Vision Creation

Initial 'SCODD Analysis' in conjunction with values contributes to the creation of mission and vision statements

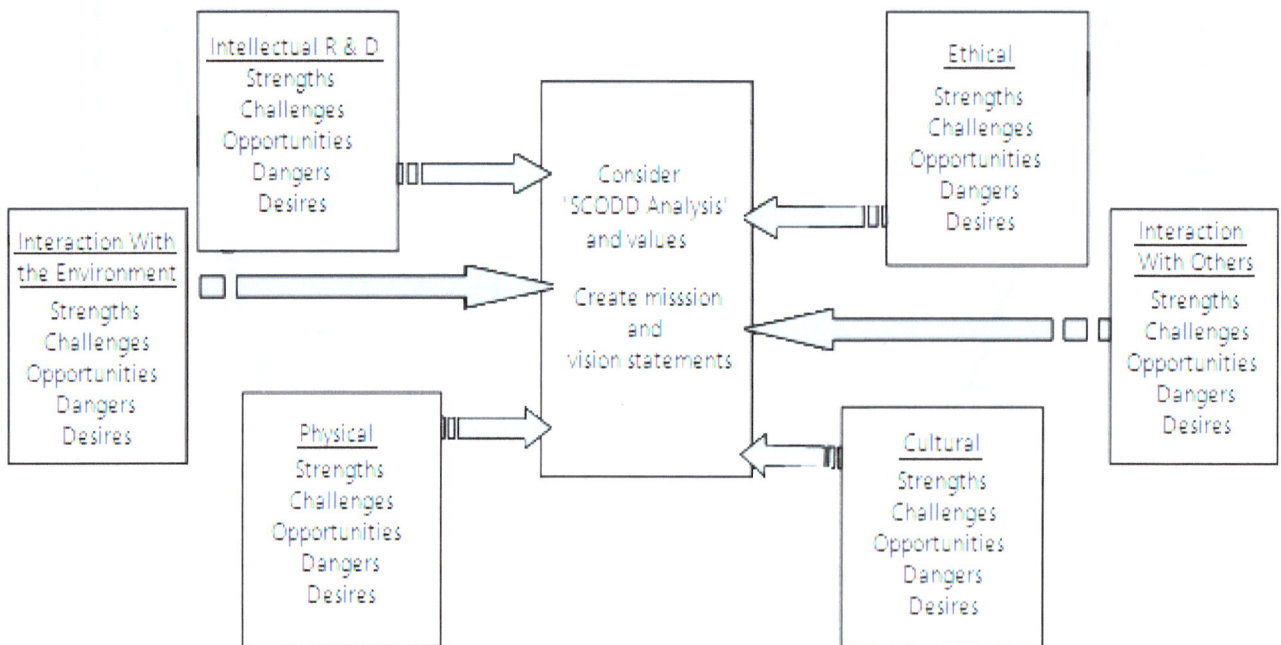

Intellectual R & D
Strengths
Challenges
Opportunities
Dangers
Desires

Ethical
Strengths
Challenges
Opportunities
Dangers
Desires

Interaction With the Environment
Strengths
Challenges
Opportunities
Dangers
Desires

Consider
'SCODD Analysis'
and values

Create misssion
and
vision statements

Interaction With Others
Strengths
Challenges
Opportunities
Dangers
Desires

Physical
Strengths
Challenges
Opportunities
Dangers
Desires

Cultural
Strengths
Challenges
Opportunities
Dangers
Desires

Value Worksheet

Make a prioritized list of what is important to your organization.
Examples may be quality, productivity, customer service or member loyalty.
This should be an indication of what is valued within the organization.

1. _____
_____

2. _____
_____

3. _____
_____

4. _____
_____

5. _____
_____

6. _____
_____

7. _____
_____

Vision and Mission Statement

Create a mission and vision statement based on the "SCODD Analysis" and values.

Vision Statement:
- Defines what the organization is or will be.
- Is short, succinct and easy to remember.
- Describes the organization in terms of its strengths, opportunities and values.
- Should elicit a clear, graphic picture of what the organization will be.
- Helps to define the mission statement.
- Visions may change and adapt based on the time frame and current circumstances.

_____

_____

_____

_____

_____

_____

_____

_____

_____

_____

Mission Statement:
- Clearly defines the purpose of the organization.
- Explains how the organization will achieve the vision using strengths, opportunities and desire.
- Describes what will be employed to achieve a goal.

_____

_____

_____

_____

_____

_____

_____

_____

_____

"SCODD Analysis" leads to values, vision and mission

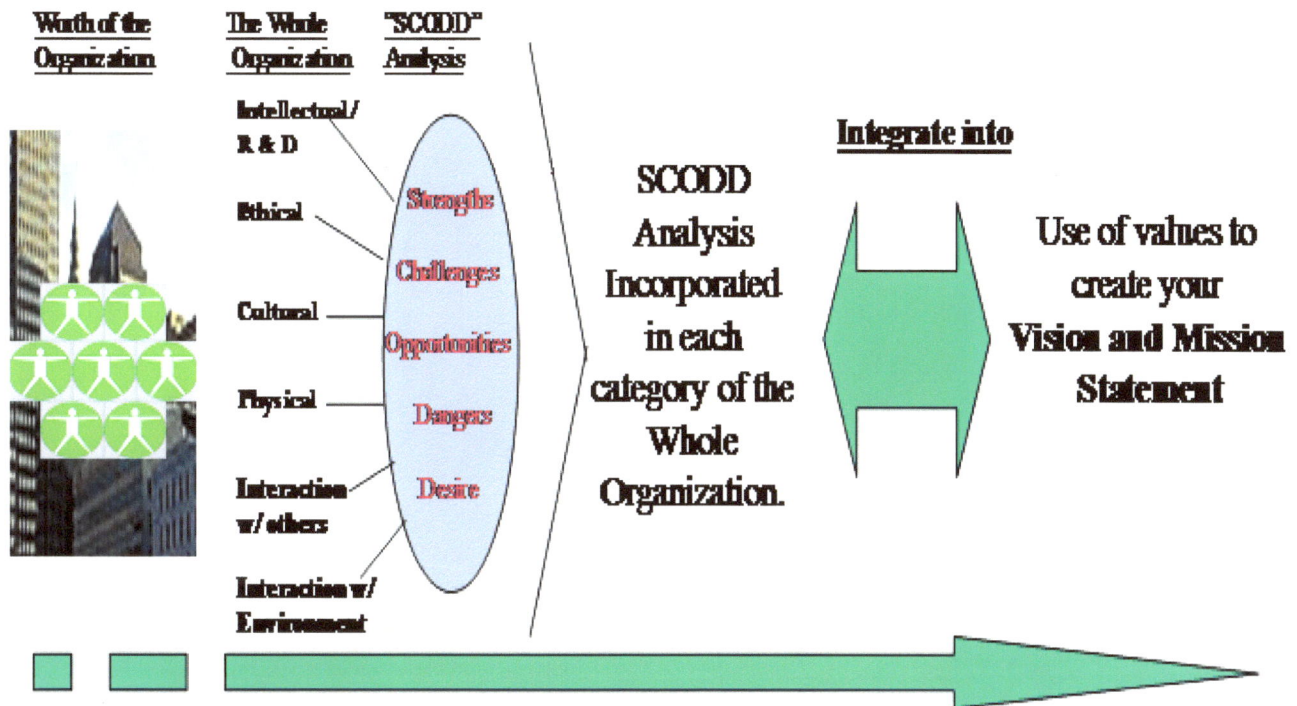

Worth of the Organization

The Whole Organization

"SCODD" Analysis

Intellectual / R & D

Ethical

Cultural

Physical

Interaction w/ others

Interaction w/ Environment

Strengths

Challenges

Opportunities

Dangers

Desire

SCODD Analysis Incorporated in each category of the Whole Organization.

Integrate into

Use of values to create your **Vision and Mission Statement**

POWER PRINCIPLE 6:

Formulate and prioritize goals using the Whole Organizational Theory.

Formation of Goals:

- Should be based on a "SCODD Analysis" of characteristics and interactions as well as on vision and mission statements. This allows goals that integrate the analysis of a present state with the declared desired state.

- Goals can be more effective if they are written, have an assigned time frame and can be measured

- The goal should be defined completely using the characteristics and interactions of the Whole Organization Theory. Some of the following may be considered:

  1. **Intellectual/research and developmental** – How will the achievement of the goal build upon or improve the underlying intellectual aspects of the organization? What new innovations will be developed?

  2. **Cultural**- What changes will be made in the culture of the organization? How will it enrich the attitudes, ideals, objectives, and behavior patterns that characterize the institution?

  3. **Physically**- What will change physically when the goal is achieved? How will present physical resources be changed or what new physical facilities will be added?

4. **Ethical**- How will the accomplishment of the goal confirm the organizations ethical standards? What will be manifest in the achievement of the goal that exemplifies the ethics of your institution?

5. **Interactions with others**- Who will be affected by the accomplishment of the goal? How will they be benefited, and how will the relationship and interaction patterns with them be changed? How will they feel about the change?

6. **Environmentally**- When the goal is completed, what will be the influence on the environment in which the organization operates? What will be the tone and character of the environment and how will this improve or facilitate the operations of the entity and the furtherance of its mission?

• The answers to the questions above will help to clearly describe the goal and sharpen the focus as to what is to be achieved.

• Once a goal is made, it can be broken down into Intermediate goals and daily steps that need to be accomplished in accordance with the mission. This will help keep focus on the goal while assisting with incremental progress towards success.

Prioritization of Goals:

- Once goals have been created, it should be determined which will promote the mission to achieve the vision the most quickly, efficiently and effectively. This goal should be worked on first.

- Accomplishment of the highest priority goal may help complete other goals, which will facilitate the mission to reach the vision.

Application:

Create and write out goals based on your organizations "SCODD Analysis," its vision and mission. Clearly define the goals in terms of the characteristics and interactions of the entity. Prioritize your goals according to which will help attain the mission and vision of the institution the most quickly, efficiently and effectively.

Goal List

Based on the "SCODD Analysis" and values, create and list goals. Prioritize them based on which will help facilitate the mission and vision the most effectively and efficiently.

☐ _____

_____ Priority# _____

☐ _____

_____ Priority# _____

☐ _____

_____ Priority# _____

☐ _____

_____ Priority# _____

☐ _____

_____ Priority# _____

☐ _____

_____ Priority# _____

☐ _____

_____ Priority# _____

☐ _____

_____ Priority# _____

Goal Definition

Select and define your highest priority goal(s) based on characteristics and interactions. Continue with the goal next in priority.

GOAL: _____   Date to be achieved _____

_____

Intellectual/Research and Developmental - Completely define your goal; envision how it will build upon your intellectual capacities and lead to innovation.

_____

_____

Cultural- What will be the culture of your organization when you accomplish your goal? How will this affect you and others?

_____

_____

Physically- Envision the physical makeup of your company. What facilities will you own and operate?

_____

_____

Ethical- What are your ethical standards? How will this affect your operations or success of your group?

_____

_____

Interactions with others- What strategic alliances will you have? How will they be affected by any changes in your organization?

_____

_____

Interactions with the environment- What will be the environment in which you operate. How will your organization affect/be benefitted from the environment?

_____

_____

Goal Worksheet

Select and clarify your highest priority goal(s) with intermediate goals and short term steps. Continue with the goal next in priority.

GOAL: _____ Date to be Achieved _____

☐ _____

_____

Intermediate Goals

☐ _____

_____

☐ _____

_____

Short Term Steps

☐ _____

_____

☐ _____

_____

☐ _____

_____

POWER PRINCIPLE 7:

Use the Whole Organizational characteristics and interactions as resources to achieve goals.

- Intellectual/Research and Developmental

- Cultural

- Physical

- Ethical

- Interactions with others

- Interactions with the environment

Application:

Use the inherent characteristics and interactions of an organization to help achieve the goal. In the "Methods and Strategies" section there are some techniques that may be used for organizations to effectively leverage their characteristics and interactions to achieve success.

One such example within the Intellectual/Research and Development Characteristic would be to do market research in order to find out what features are in demand for a certain product. This may facilitate a goal to create a product with new features that would provide 100,000 sales.

"SCODD Analysis" and Goal Formulation

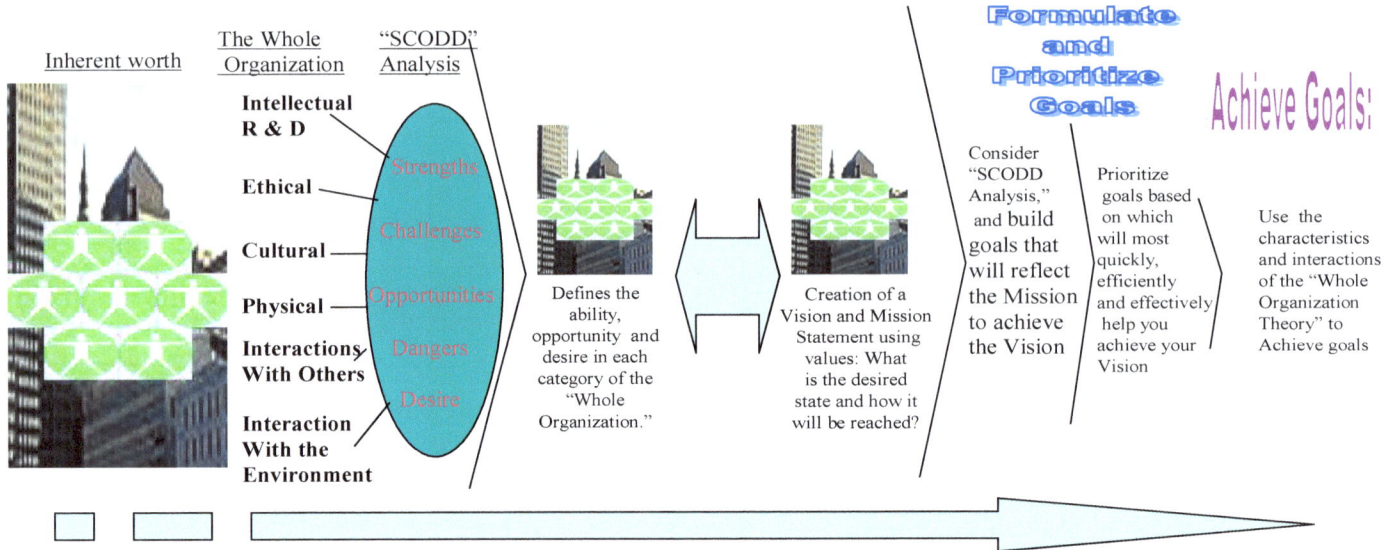

Inherent worth

The Whole Organization

"SCODD" Analysis

Intellectual R & D

Ethical

Cultural

Physical

Interactions With Others

Interaction With the Environment

Strengths

Challenges

Opportunities

Dangers

Desire

Defines the ability, opportunity and desire in each category of the "Whole Organization."

Creation of a Vision and Mission Statement using values: What is the desired state and how it will be reached?

Formulate and Prioritize Goals

Achieve Goals:

Consider "SCODD Analysis," and build goals that will reflect the Mission to achieve the Vision

Prioritize goals based on which will most quickly, efficiently and effectively help you achieve your Vision

Use the characteristics and interactions of the "Whole Organization Theory" to Achieve goals

Methods and Strategies

On the following pages are some methods that may be
used to effectively leverage characteristics
and interactions to achieve success.

Intellectual/Research and Developmental

- Encouragement and compensation for organizational members and those in the research and development department to come up with new and innovative ways to accomplish the vision of the institution may be employed.

- Use of current research available through journals, trade publications and the internet to learn about what it will take to most effectively reach a goal can be highly effective.

- Obtaining or encouraging others to gain higher levels of education and training may provide greater perspectives and insights into how a goal may be accomplished more efficiently and effectively.

Cultural

- All members of the organization should know and understand the mission and vision of the institution, and the values and principles upon which they are based.

- Greater cooperation may be achieved if all members understand the goals of entity, why they have been set and how they relate to the vision and mission.

- Communication to the members of an organization explaining how the mission, vision and goals of the organization include, relate to and benefit them is essential.

- An explanation of what role and responsibilities each member has in attaining the mission, vision and goals of the organization can be very helpful. Rewards for pro-activity and efforts that work towards each are also effective.

- Helping each member know that they are important and their contributions are valued is essential.

Physical

- Technology can sometimes greatly increase the efficiency and effectiveness of an organization. Updates in technology should be assessed to determine whether the cost is outweighed by what can be accomplished towards attaining the mission, vision and goals of the organization.

- A complete understanding of all available resources and how they are used should be encouraged for all members who have access to them. Proficiency for users should be required to take full advantage of available resources.

- New and more efficient ways to use existing resources should be explored.

- Maintenance and current upkeep of resources may reduce costs and allow financial resources to be used for other purposes that further the mission.

Ethical

- Greater efforts to communicate the ethics of an organization as it works towards its vision may engender respect by its members and others outside the institution. This may lead to greater support for the accomplishment of its purpose.

- Remaining ethical, even while change is taking place, will confirm to those who are affected that the values of the organization remain the same as it embraces innovation. This may facilitate retention and loyalty, which will reduce recruiting and training costs.

- Ethics can help guide and expedite vital decisions that may promote the completion of goals and the mission of the organization.

Interactions with Others

- Consultants and coaches can provide new perspectives, greater insight and expertise that will speed the completion of goals.

- Synergies inherent in cooperation between two contributors can provide a greater ability to accomplish a purpose than if the contributors act individually.

- Cooperation between interested parties sometimes yields access to resources, other advantages and benefits not available to individual entities.

- When an organization works to make sure interactions with others outside the institution are positive and beneficial, it may lead to referrals, word of mouth endorsements and positive feedback. This can promote progress towards the organizations mission as well as unite members towards the realization of their objectives.

Interaction with the Environment

- An organization should strive to learn about its environment and its resources. An effort should be undertaken to learn how these resources may inherently assist the organization in reaching its objectives. How certain resources can be adapted to aid in the entity's mission is also important to consider.

- An institution should also learn how to adapt to its environment and adjust to make use of resources available.

- Obstacles within an environment can sometimes be turned into opportunities. With a different perspective and innovation, some obstacles may be approached in a new way to create opportunities not previously considered. Different or more efficient ways to use resources may be included in such transformations.

- Organizations can create cues within its internal environment such as images, symbols and written statements that will remind members of the entity's mission, vision and goals. This creates an atmosphere that is conducive to the joint attainment of each.

- Institutions can influence the environment through advertising, public press releases and even community involvement. This may help create an atmosphere that is conducive to the objectives of the organization.

References

Carnegie, D. (author), Pell, A.R., & Carnegie, D. (editors).
(1982). <u>How to Win Friends and Influence People.</u>
New York: Simon and Schuster.

Carnegie, D. (author), & Carnegie, D. (editor). (1984)
<u>How to Stop Worrying and Start Living.</u> New York: Simon and
Schuster.

Covey, S. (1989) <u>The Seven Habits of Highly Effective
People.</u> New York: Simon and Schuster.

"Quotations Database" <u>Motivational Quotes.com Web Site</u>
June 2001. Online http://www.motivationalquotes.com

Devore, S. (1984) <u>The Neuropsychology of Achievement.</u>
Audio book Newark, CA: Sybervision Systems incorporated.

Ziglar, Z. (1998) <u>Breaking Through to the Next Level.</u>
Tulsa,OK: Honor Books.

About the author

Scott Newberger learned about setting and achieving goals at an early age when he decided he wanted to try out for the high school football team although he had never played any organized sports. He had been heavy set as a boy and was always picked last during any athletic endeavors. Through his faith in God and with the help of friends and family, Scott was excited to reach his goal and made the second of two freshman football teams, even though he was last string. Prayers and hard work helped him improve and by the end of the year he was starting. Eventually he started on varsity and became the captain of the high school football team.

This and other events helped Scott to believe that dreams can be achieved. He also learned the process that allows success.

Scott is currently the President and CEO of Lifecharge Consulting, a firm dedicated to strategic coaching for organizations and individuals. He is a portfolio consultant for a major brokerage firm and sits on the Board of Directors for R. W. Meyer Company, one of the largest privately owned land management companies in Hawaii. Scott has a Masters in Business Administration, a Masters in Innovative Leadership, a Bachelors Degree in Psychology and is an Accredited Asset Management Specialist.

Scott enjoys teaching and has spoken in front of hundreds. He holds a College Teaching Certificate and has taught Community College of the Air Force Certified Classes. As Technical Sergeant of the Arizona Air National Guard, he's been involved in project management and has been a certified trainer and instructor.

During his free time Scott enjoys spending time with his wife and children. He is an Elder in The Church of Jesus Christ of Latter-Day Saints where he works as a youth leader. Scott is a Black Belt in Karate and is a Certified Sports Mental Training Coach.

Through Lifecharge PowerPac © and Lifecharge Organizational PowerPac ©, Scott wishes to help individuals and organizations reach their full potential. He believes through proper analysis and strategic goal setting, higher levels of achievement can be attained than had afore been considered possible.

www.ingramcontent.com/pod-product-compliance
Lightning Source LLC
Chambersburg PA
CBHW052048190326
41521CB00002BA/144